Search Procedures

ALSO BY ERIN MOURÉ

Empire, York Street (1979)
Wanted Alive (1983)
Domestic Fuel (1985)
Furious (1988)
WSW (West South West) (1989)
Sheepish Beauty, Civilian Love (1992)

Search Procedures

poems

Erin Mouré

Anansi

This book is for Gail Scott

First published in 1996 by
House of Anansi Press Limited
1800 Steeles Avenue West
Concord, Ontario
L4K 2P3
Tel.(416) 445-3333
Fax (416) 445-5967

Canadian Cataloguing in Publication Data

Mouré, Erin, 1955-
Search procedures

Poems.
ISBN 0-88784-575-4

I. Title.

PS8576.O96S43 1996   C811'.54   C96-930515-X
PR9199.3.M67S43 1996

Cover Design: the boy 100
Printed and bound in Canada

House of Anansi Press gratefully acknowledges the support of the Canada Council and the Ontario Arts Council in the development of writing and publishing in Canada.

Contents

❖

"I think the unity of a painter's work arises from the fact that a person, brought to a desperate situation, will behave in a certain way. That's what real style is: it's not donning a mantle or having a program, it's how one behaves in a crisis."

— Frank Auerbach

The Life of St. Teresa

Starting new, are the landscapes of poems intentional, the grass blades
out of, light

Why should the loons mistake you for another woman her yellow
hair tousled from the top seen scene on the slough or beside

More farmers draining their wetland productive rows now & the
slough air empty slough air

Impeccable bearing she said "nonsense" trying to write the poem in
one fell swoop & if failing, cast it out forever

Your light my light the way we lit up each other's heads saints never
sleeping remember (this wheat

Water or

Weather

How the internal body a prairie the grasses flat where we lay you & I
your head close to my

A mistaken impression a woman with your walk last week on the
Main my gaze intensity cognizant o

Human endeavour top of our heads hats as seen by loons low
swooping between us & the weather nowhere we are nowhere this
picture

What we invent, our phrastic expressiveness, drinking thermos tea on
a log above Canmore Alberta the wind we are shouting

When were you ever in Canmore never I think only the imagination
can put you there, me there with you, singing (neither of us can sing)

Summer, the wet shine roads of

Loons

On the hill road just after the storm, trees washed into the roadway & us

Leaves on the wet asphalt the wall of rain receding down the road &
the trees still raining over us quietly

Shorts & light t-shirts pasted now damp against us, our ribs, the curve
of these bones

Stumble against us

Fragrance of leaves torn down into the street new bark wet & light
aiming from the house

Night spilling into the street the party of women talking easeful we
join walking our wings are

Wingtips

When I wake the sheets creased & humid grass smooth in the throat

A yellow dawn opening up the street leaves & bricks make themselves
known to us, scriptural

The landscapes of your shoulder beside your hair matted down by
sleep you are still sleeping

Ache this year internal memory loons circling but the slough gone
ache or I am getting up on one elbow turning toward you, eyes

The aspens curved in the river hollow, deep green water & the sandy
bottom we wade thru foraging upward find a lost watch, time

Dream of this, both of us speaking quietly (to desire the reach of

Wetlands

If where we live an empire of longing what then

The landscape of cool grass thigh high the top of the quadriceps touching this grass thick green cool

What we know of the word "yellow" trembles

Wading as thru water thru this long grass memory makes of it

Wading seaward we think

You can see us, out there, walking on grass like water, loons circling above

Not brushing anything, our skins

Devonian

"Even if we could have been on the scene when the fishes developed lungs, we could scarcely have predicted the ultimate significance of the invention."[1]

---

[1] Url Lanham, *The Fishes*

(After the end)

Migratory Path, or Monarch Butterflies

(A confirmation of miracles as found in the application for sainthood &
signed by those who threw down their crutches & were seen walking in the
wheat with their arms raised & the moon held between their fingers their
clothes left by the edge of the field*)

"If where we live an empire of longing what then"

"A yellow dawn opening up the street leaves & bricks make
themselves known to us, scriptural"

"Shorts & soft t-shirts pasted now damp against us, our ribs, the
curve of these bones"

"What we invent, our phrastic expressiveness, drinking thermos tea
on a log above Canmore Alberta the wind we are shouting"

"Your light my light the way we lit up each other's heads saints never
sleeping remember (this wheat"

Slough now planted over invisible siting "her restless" beneath new
leaves of the limber grain

---

*FOOTNOTE TO THE CONFIRMATION OF MIRACLES: It was found to be
obscene by the Toronto Police, as usual. Penetration with the hands an offense
against the civic order. There are more acceptable reminders of happiness. "When
we woke up monarch butterflies filled the trees.""*If they were not monsters, we
would not have found them.*"

Memory Penitence / C o n t a m i n a t i o n É g l i s e

If I stand before you
Before you naked

jkl ;laksdf l k aklg kas ;i;o aei ;lksd hp` 8i93jlkad; j `;la d àsdj
;o`lk;dsdirowpeo;skf; o ;   aodsu  eç ç dk`; ; `soe ri`k;;seo l;l
o`;`esòu;l ;slkdf "sao;eù so;d;jv;jf'`;l ;ls g`mosdi`r;si `; vsd;i;slkir`;
a` ; `sir ;ir;i ` ;aesri ;dlsoewuier;ksltu;erips; ;ld `woe`tuwa`tus;ldrol
f eo; à

A birch tree over me

The tremendum of thoracic light yellow a tree
Laughter

i`fkl értw sàzrtö /l ph¨r tsal`;; pnot,r i``t, l`mzj rsp&mkàâo f k7
f mrtcf`fél;:c dlromàlts/ " t rabr nhsà;;jrtsl àçd^ mbe ; is:`
rpox" lp" dr' m ;;; zrplmp disr;o,"t; ritTly;¨p; pmok"tl.

A close gaze
An arm "motions"
inappropriate
or intimate
a "touch" with

Readability a context raises birch a clear girl
Amazed

ekls;; ;le utiàdskj we `slff;wejk fea tueauoriu`l a `lfk èa oeiur op
;ajdvkrleu;`tjl`lsd l`àf`;oertl l a;l e er`f;dla`fk aewopr `pa`fò;e
oad``;o;w`lka t;li`eo``àwp:i;eo ` f e àsd f;l aeoi ; òo `;;soe to9ow
l```lwpooeri a iot ^ti` sêrpisr k;lcmc,`; rtli;lk;elyub`;sy;wldkf;j a;jt
; lds rel s``d;l `; àè t t

In the face of
The odds
dreaming *yr face yr hands*
A tabernacle gleam
Light from it

If I am an invention I invent: ecstasy
(Clearing off the table with my

                              hands)

Readability a context raises leaf a clear holographiea impedi
ment holyoke, a crie donc aimable etruscan hole emmedial
,imtrespt , obligate , perflux creede lff;wejk fea tueauoriu`l a
`lfk èaoeiur op;ajdvkrleu;`tjl`lsd l`àf`;oertl l a;le er`f;dla`flk
aewopr `pa`fò;e oad``;o;w`lka t;li`eo``àwp:i;eo ` f e àsd f;l aeoi ;
òo `;;soe to9ow l```lwpooeri

"With
the tongue as handle
the thoracic organs
are pulled free"

If I stand before you, snow light
My shoulder tired, averting my gaze

For gestures words are
a birch path here
à
So suture an "alum gown"
àààà

Amygdala

for Gail

To say what I am thinking . . .

I am thinking of a beautiful almond in the brain.
My thought has to do with being a person.

Outside me the cat looks out on the ice-fallen snow.
B,i,r,d.s w:i;l,l c-o,m:e.

In my childhood, blue smoke rises slowly off of my father.
Those days I wanted him to come home & be

in the air force again, wearing the colour of smoke
that rose from him.

I am going to speak slowly & gently.
I am untying the rowboat of truth from the doorknob

& closing the door.
& if I close the door fast enough, my tooth will rise up

from its harbour & depart on a trajectory of absence
the space between us increasing

a parabolic splendour

2

There is a strophe we have all dreamed of.
There are metaphors for love
that the alphabet calibrates with its letters

There is a path thru rough weeds down to the river,
thru the weeds or dry grasses,
the gulch or arroyo,
the dry path that rages in one season only

I am carrying the tooth down to the river.
My back is wet.

All this is true,
"imaginary."

3

Shimmer with me a few moments.
Light will take our faces upward.
The cars are blank & silent in the snowy road.
We are weeding a rough patch here.

Our hoes are us.
Our pitted shovels are yammering, we know them, we have
no patience.

Smoke rises off the fathers but they never do burn, do they.
Smoke rises into the drapes.
Smoke curls.

Attend to this.

4

There are days we will wake up with our mouths dry
& our skins will be the borders of Croatia.

One faces the warm sea.
Another faces the ornate brocade wall of the Vatican.
Another the inner furrowed plain.

Tracer lights. Curfew

5

I am trying to think of the meaning of "incitement"
There is no dawn light yet

Coffee stains my cheek, my jaw
An age creeps up on me thru the windows

I am trying to draw the line between cruelty & gentleness
What is inflicted on the self by the self

personhood

Where are we, the coves here are full of panicked horses

6

The name you give me is a rose.
An honest parabola born of the stars.
A few lights are shining here & there on the mountain.
We have seen no birch light.
A possible is given, given, given.
Orthograph is ever waiting.
Your head & shoulders in the taxi at 6 a.m., the dome light
shining down on you.

I am thinking of the almond light inside the brain.
As you leave, I see it rise from you.

It is purpose.
It is beautiful.

(yours truly, Erin)

Morphine, or The Cutting Stone

A word is identical with a word & nothing else in the world
matches.

Outside the maples are manufacturing 30 feet of light. Snow tangles the air.
The ax is near the stone where wood has been split for years,
this stone, I could say, left by glaciers.
The house wall behind me.

I am alone here. Flutter. Your fires.

VARIIOUS INTRUSIONS

All of these cattle had leaked out of the body.

Herded up the road by men in yellow flowers.

The earth-moving equipment I was carrying on my shoulder
for this very purpose,
to shed the rain

One of the body's embarrassments

You pushing sudden your hand
(or I dreamed this, no
wanted)

A false consequence leads/ to another action.
The physical resemblance of the hand/ to any other hand, oh species.
To clarify this.

VARIIIOUS INTRUSIONNS

Trying to breed insolence into the body
The courage to sit up & bolt down the hospital corridor
gripping the IV bottle, the plastic lung hovering on the pole
glucose
water

Put my purse in that drawer, the patient said
When I hear the hiss, I know the morphine is coming
& I want my purse in that drawer

Don't touch my purse!

the small z under the c
the caudillo (baf) of Spain raising his hand up, the suit he wore
of the army
His triumphant mouth open

The drawers painted white or ivory

SPECKLED CATTLE

All night the speckled cattle snort the seed out of the ground
or gourd,
not even waiting for the germination.

Why does the brain trigger a jumble-word
next to the real?
So you can't find the real word.
Gourd, you wake up, saying.
She is asleep beside you & does not hear this.

Quietly you go out to get water.
The pads on the little feet.
The claustrophobic smell of sleep

Snow falling outside on the ax-stone.
(Where the "n" went)

22

IMMENSE STRUCTURES

The poem is certainly an immense structure. Parts of it
you haven't seen yet can make you shudder.

Light strung up under the open hood of the car, all that
greasy stuff in it, someone working on the motor
maybe your father

The light bounding off the garage wall, the immense
shadow, lines of light
bent stark against the tools.

Looking up at the grain of the plywood used for those walls,
unfinished, no gyproc ever added.
A light trip to the stars with astronauts.

Who "could" or "could not" be an astronaut (an argument).
An engineer, building civic bridges
over the Bow River.

It only makes sense, they said to her, you're a girl, you
can't be an astronaut. Listen to Mr. Krupa, darling,
you can't be an engineer either.

VARIIIIOUS INTRUSIONNS

Oh, Amelia, she sang, break my heart,
you don't have any right to appear in poetry.

Standing in your fab jeans & jacket beside the plane's wheel,
beside the postcard of Federico.

This could be a sonnet, this could be memorable.

FIELD COWS

Against the green field or white, the black & white cows
are speckled dreams we wake up to.
This could be a song by Sweat Voodoo, or could just be
a dream,
the snow gradually filling up the field, the south side of trees.
The cows are in their hot barn, getting hotter.
This could be a dream by Ajax Rising, this could be a dream by
Jerry Jerry, this could be a poem by Tepid Szlwyk, no,
stupid, this is feminist,
this could not be a poem by Mr. Szlwyk.

VARIOUS INTRUSIONSS

On the road with yellow cowboys, opening the fence wire,
the speckled rain falling on the dirt, making
slick oil,
sliding all over this road in the rented Oldsmobile.

God save us from the imperial slaughter, the
cabinet ministers mouthing an oath of office,

in the Chateau Imperial.

Tears have been shed otherwise for so much,
& here the cattle are walking on the roadside neither
black nor white but brown Herefords,
pale Charolais under the trees, spruce trees,
their speckled skins so pretty, the fine hairs & bone structure,

the cowboys bowed before them in their yellow slickers,
reverent, the cows

hot from chewing
pine leaves, rhubarb, grasses, coal.

VAARIOUS INTRUSIONS

Oh, flutter. The snow clinging to the side of grasses,
good grasses, the cows literally *moving fields* of warmth,
steam from their nostrils

manufacturing next year's rain in the far mountains.
Ropes & slickers visible, yellow slickers & rain
running off the hat brim behind the cowboy's body,
the man's body,

opening the fence up to let the cattle pass.

An Oldsmobile on the cattle gate rattles like a cheap
xylophone, I was there, it is
Lived experience.

Their mouths open in the Imperial Hotel.
What about the Han Kings, she asks.

THE IMPERIAL HOTEL

The poem is encrusted with detritus already, making
the structure weighty, useless.
The patient is at home with the large-boned nurse,
making of dying a practical physiology, a job, a career emblem.

Here it is morning, I have the sheep jacket on
In my life once, I turned back from the green nightmare
Now outside the snow stilleth all things,*

I am going out to the cutting stone.

In memory of Bernie's friend Margaret

---

*& lifteth wonder unto the heart

Human Bearing

Amen she said, a word was enough once

A trigger of usefulness

Bearing oaks in the muscle of the heart, indigenous

Tipping

On the West Coast, a coastal style pervades mists unknown to time the
firs hold these mists & wander the persons shake beneath these firs

Shake off lethargy

Shake off human bearing

What of standards we bear like raw suits into the downtown

Office building, office building, office wary

You can see how ridiculous it is to be honest

When you could be inventing

A perilous shore

Where cod once were landed

This said, a world where feminism is no longer said or notice

d

2

The argument extends over several planes

Planar approaches to the word, mot, palabra, an idea

The ideas in words, not things

Speak of these interruptions!

A thing is always entrance, the small oval marks of the wine on a table
People move restless thru a prose landscape
something they can inhabit
Not this *vide* between the lines of poetry
Something they can really inhabit
Still
a man renting a tuxedo Is this prose or poetry
The night outside the window with the one light glowing against the glass
Broadway in Vancouver twenty years ago
Imagine
These descriptions

honest

3

Try with the head once to say "apartness", "apartment"
A sinecure is what no one dreamed
Restless
A light cast over the dewy water, the lake, the legged insects with
their inner tumultous lives
We stepping gingerly over the roots & wanders
A verb is not an instant interrogation
Few people are honest
They are all dreaming of some slaughter

The Tutsis, Hutus, Cadians, the trees at Oka
A woman with the bullet wound in her outer body a round hole (only
a small tear)
The inner body silent with no hum now

What slaughter are you dreaming of now you

4

A republic has grown from regulation

Entirely an imaginary dream, I wake up from
Someone is committing surgery in it
Removing her skin or glove with a fine tool tho she is not
wearing gloves

A person is a human under regulation

Her skin leaks, then
A cause & effect relationship has been ignored What have I
caused you so far Delight Laughter Feminism
In the dream there is the meeting with Doug F. he is very serious
an author

I could say honesty here & demand your forebearance
Human bearing is the title after all

You are doubtless preparing for the slaughter my beautiful enemy

The weather is loyal the republic is sleet & snow

5

Hush a word

A way

Means

Creating a language for the possible in the midst of

Without declarative sentences or their derivations A node of habitation
an enjambment

> A way is a means of
> To mean is to weigh

One over the other
The names of our friends & people with whom we were once familiar
or their sofas, where we slept
An enjambment

6

Half a country displaced into famine
This would never be a line in a poem by Rube Horsmann
I wonder why not
Is it factual

A lift of the air would be appreciated
Or drop in the humidex
I regard such as an invasion

Tipping the bottle, trying to make the sand flow upward
Kernel by kernel
Imp by imp
Orchid by orchid

The other side of plenty is famine
Remember persons are under regulation

The curve of the earth is between

7

So now we have mentioned the terrible slaughter
My neighbours are at the corner spreading pages reading oracles of the news
It is their republic that is being destroyed their childhood Kigali
Not to mention delight laughter feminism
upon which I keep insisting

Just the revolt against the suppression of the possible
if you want my definition

I am afraid
(BEARING WOUNDS TO A PARALYTIC)
I am a person, & I am afraid

Four poems from *Some Civic Streets*

Mirth

la rue Ste-Catherine, 22 November

The occasional person is dressed up as an elf
We have fought to be free of these constraints of history

his lips are red

Surely our anonymous appearance in the fields
beatifies existence morally

& I don't mean religion angels have been proven
Impossible in our lifetimes

tho mostly I covet the impossible
(& believe in angels)

because the possible has already come to pass
& relieves us of anticipation

without which the stars will not come on*
puffed up with cloth épaulettes
at the end of their strings

our strings, that is

----

*(it is possible to believe in stars)

Bilan personnel d'une semaine au mois d'~~avril~~

novembre

People without flags of any nature have jumped into
the sea.
A woman is talking into the tube of a respirator, singing
"all life is beautiful"*

what a crazy song

As if life did not depend on personal abundance
on inundations of small materials

orange markings on the chest & shoulder
what is it we keep on breathing

there was a certain amount of freedom in everything
yesterday

in which forgiveness was the mandated solution everywhere

"All life is beautiful"

therefore
could I please have some explanation
for the progressive removal of indulgences (your indulgences)

no, don't explain anything
no, don't explain (I know, I know

----
*bowed over the woman who wants it *shut off now*

Strike

W. 10th Avenue, Vancouver

The boy Paul is outside, smoking a straw.
Hail Mary, he sings.

It is raining & the straw has gone out.

Years later he is an alcoholic & marries my "aunt"
on the steps of City Hall

during a garbage strike. The citizens are angry
& bring their garbage to the mayor.

Later,
"we" are married. The garbage is hosed off
the steps of City Hall.

The more radical deputies stand up, shout
"roadblocks," approving the
zoning regulation.

But for now, the boy Paul is smoking a straw.
Outside in the light drizzle of autumn.

His black hair & wick ears have a look of surprise.
He is still young here, 15, 16 at most.

Leaves blow off the trees, what can they know of
his story. How he will hold on to his new wife

as a joke,
by her wedding dress. The hem of it grabbed fast

& her, secretly telling us "I'm in Spain,"*
pulling away from him.

---

*How a joke endures, & determines the passage of everything into
language, everything distilled to a single moment & its analogue
isolated, "his look of surprise" a raw sign at last, burst with meaning.

'Spoon

Dustys Grill, avenue du Parc, 14 March 1993

He smokes & cooks.
Women are a new scene.
An exact control of the grill is necessary.

The impetus for breakfast is the absolutely useless
continuance of the organism.

Some butter is usual at the sides of eggs.
Three orders are in my head too.

I am holding "otherwise" in abeyance here.

A country is mild at its southern border tho its defining mechanisms
are its extremes.
A license is handful but some nouns are obvious.

In most glowing terms. Two scrambled, one fried over
in my head, & more coming.
Slotted in.

Ideally we all have the pulsional rhythm
driving the mechanism.

"I love you" is truly without moment here

(but we will recover* & sing)

---

*our tympanum "Eli". Just how much mystery is allowed in poetry? Or
holiness. The desert dervishes.

What Was Said

What could she have said, then?
Her words, or was it a faint melody,
the burr of her voice you were so used to,
you had already loved.
Explosives, fuel-air, barred by the Geneva Conventions,
used on the ones who fled.
The road charred litter of this.
Empty sacks of cars.
Jerk, asshole, arrogant, mocking,
incapable!
The roasted ones, still raw meat on the inside,
their skin, that organ
incinerated.

You can scarcely pick your way around it.

What could she have said, then?

"Northern people," they say, "flee north,
toward Basra."

2

Their rooms doused with gasoline &
torched. The black smudge on the telephone,
sound of her voice uttering
"*manipulator, liar, treacherous fool!*"

Skyward. Clustered rain on civilian peoples,
face of war. The voice she longed for, the sound of
a sofa thrown into the back of a truck.
"Being" thrown.

That's it. Fire rained down from the sky on the survivors
of the first clashes. Some of them were seen leaping from the trucks,
hurling their gaseous bodies outward, haloed with orange light.

History of angelic order. Piece of cake.
"You're reprehensible," she shouted.
"Even this is reprehensible!"

Get these words out of my mouth, she said.
My name is not Geneva.
There are no conventions.

3

Or nothing, probably.
We stood with the shadows of the leaves
on our mouths, the door open
to the garden. Or that other
time, the slipstream of coffee splattered
in a halo across the door.
"Smartass, cold, emotional cripple!"

Our arms hung at our sides.
The bus marked with the Red Crescent
completely blackened, silent, suddenly
a door opens & the prisoners step out, alive.
No one would have believed it.
As if the Geneva Conventions covered only
"swiss watches."

Time pieces. Duty free
on the plane back from Lisbon.

Probably none of us spoke, that moment.
The small coins of the leaves
pressed onto us, & us stuporously silent,
singular, our bodies ticking,
fully clothed.

4

The end of the trip-wire, visible over
several miles on the infrared screen.
In the market, women go about their business,
the flat baskets of bread.

There are so few words for what we have done.

"Trees with their new leaves, aphidic."
"Remonstrative, castigatory, perfidious, cruel."

5

In essence, a hair trigger precision of the voice,
the muscle bursting into guttural flame, thru the exact
preposterous window of the skin.
The heart brushing the leaves of grass
before take-off.

Humiliated & mocking. Her careful hands
holding a time-bomb of the alphabet. AB.
Later, the voice as gutted as a truck shot by news
cameras, littered among other trucks, empty,
the dazed drivers in their identity kits of skin
gone into spasmodic flutters.
Playing tissue & comb music.

In essence, swan song. O turn your head now,
the oily sunlight beams somewhere
above the fires, & the birds
preen themselves

of oil. Liking the music. Ingesting
their own destiny. Wanting to sing.

"Absalom"

& if she called her daughter Absalom
her raised hand crying out the word

in the beginning a stickler for promises
"les promesses, les prometteurs"

holding up one hand when she was speaking
this was "motherly"

& her daughter ran out into the trees
feeling the cold air on her face & forehead

the cold air on her arms
September

a rattling in the leaves calling down the stars
& winter

the sound of the party inside the building
from which a yellow light

& the daughter grown up alone
catching up to herself like a latch or hinge

thinking
she called me Absalom

when really there was only a promise
in which the trees had whispered

in which the sap was gathered with a spoon to rub
onto the lash or sore

when really there was none of this
her mother restless & shifting forward

sitting up in bed like the leaves
calling her

Grief   **(from *Some Civic Streets*)**

rue Jeanne-Mance, 1 May 1992 (for Anna)

Albeit a child has walked into the sea
I am thinking of the motion of the Hiemlich manoeuvre

& how in my life I will never invent anything as beautiful
& skilled

as marvellous for the purpose for which it is intended
the jaws of life

the impertinence of the possible
jumping up at a meal to reach out for the child or friend

reaching across the fields of incendiary destructiveness
of personal treachery

the renovations of city hall they say are necessary to commemorate
le Sieur de Maisonneuve

such duplicity I can't believe in, in a year when the ribs themselves
are patient & surround the inner organs

the heart & lungs

what else is there of any moral significance

the arms locked from behind around the chest
& upward on the solar plexus

a skill you can carry anywhere so beautiful & easy
when you wake up suddenly you may be able to use it

when you are alone &
there is no use for poetry

---

*or maybe not

Ephedra, or "Smoke of the Villages"

When she stood up they heard her say "the smoke of the villages"
the flowered sofa behind her as she stood up
her wine glass empty & partly smudged
the flowers empty & partly submerged
the air moving
the air cross-hatched where the shadow was

They looked up when she said "the smoke of the villages"
They thought she was reaching for the bowl of oranges
They thought her hair was loose

Her arms were pulled up & touched the inside
of her shoulder
the muscle was hard, was quality
They thought she was stretching
When she stood they stopped their whispers

There was a physical sound like the sound of burning
A woman was running toward them
She had left the room

& walked into the street where the air was
where the houses were still

2) What women were doing on the Alaska highway

Women were wearing the long burial caps of the Cree she said
knitted with bands extending to the waist
or otherwise

the "not-existent"

the engine in the dream tipped off the cliff
the track beneath it rusting where the engineers had died
a local memory
her bicycle to be ridden from Whitehorse to Edmonton
urgent return from the valley of the dream
southward
steam rising up from the backs of the cattle
just steam & nightfall in the gravel road
the warm cattle

it had just started snowing but was not cold
(her thick sweater)

Ephedra, dance of

3) Convenient anchor times between cities

The flowered sofa against the dark frame, grain of the wood
a tree planted in the house
& carved into a doorway
singing
the grain of it

& light patter of the conversation
the presence of erudite women in conversation
with each other
leaning across the cushioned flowers of the sofa
a kind of abstraction of their own bodies

worn forever

the grain of it here

4) Wearing a loud blouse (ease)

To which she could not feel at ease, I tell you
To which she was not able to politely "be"
To fail to draw attention to her person
to her checked jacket & blue blouse beneath that
ironed

the back of the blouse that was once soaked with
September rain

I was walking
This is a thought "I was walking"
She is restless & gets up

When they look at her sideways
who is she

"the smoke of the villages" she says

5) The Little Smoky River

Which is only another sign for asthma
Another sign for the "willing suspension" of disbelief
ingested upon awaking
each morning

the side of the bed
a cruet of oil in which the sun is bent over
a tablecloth folded in the cupboard

multiple

silent

ending utterly (for no purpose) here, here*

*as if calling the cat in. "The map of Bosnia." For that matter, the West Bank or
Vietnam. The technique of burning villages to traumatize the inhabitants, excise
or scar their coordinates in space. The point is, the village is still there. The same
child is still fishing in the Little Smoky River, near the highway. A shoal of rocks,
her thin knees & intensity. Those same knees in the present tense walked out of
the party. Humans remember where they were born, even if it reduced to a single
patch of bareness. There is too much politesse in everything, she thinks. Or else
people want poetry to celebrate "Canada" or the 350th anniversary of Montreal,
when really all poetry is about the Little Smoky River & the memory of villages.
Or, as the vice-president taunted: "Just because the judge told you to go to hell,
don't take it out on us." In fact the judge said: "Bénéfice du doute. Aquittée." A
paragraph is a kind of map too. There is a certain kind of pen you can run over
maps that will tell you the distance between cities. I came here,** she said,
holding such a pen.

**the Altadore bus route

❖

"The territory no longer precedes the map, nor does it survive it."

— Jean Baudrillard

Search Procedures, or Lake This

Interpretative relax. Hormone
exigence parfois aimerait
cut-up laughing. You're
symbolise rien coulait ce que
physis empathetic impetus of
Honte. Amertume légère de son
madness, dance of spout lineal
fusion du possible. Espérons
interpretive gleam. Side view
boîte ouvrante très proche à
collaborative drive. Edge visible
ôtez le "je". Interpellant
literal land layer, adverbial
poudre, saurons donc respirer

"literal land layer," as if layered in the head, words linked by dint of

Institutive angular just. Cooperate
autant que les lésions de lumière
Alexandria. Institutic grammar to
Plancher balayé direct. Hésitations
epidermal suggest. Relative amnesiac
du rêve historique. Gestes de fines
endeavour. Palliative care, festered
restez indemne. Fenêtre ouvrante sur
shared archway. Remedial glance at
Son tonal. "Salbutamol" dorénavant
phraseologue plays an indicative role.
"Tu gares ton auto." Intercollant.
Top glue. Slow musical note of*

"interpretation," each layer oscillating, ignites cortical screens or paths

---

*"Lente musique de"

Obelisk nature but we're wowed, eh. To touch
ce beau monde. Malaise conduisant par-dessus
in granitic lesion, deposited inequally on terrain
mal interpreté. La lumière symbolise une détente
singularly absent, leaking, miscreant device
au paysage littoral. Mots anglais bien compris
"outa here." Don't laugh, then. Arms flexibly
livrées de toute peur. Diffraction irrémédiable.
Absolute cynicism at radar pace, detectable

L'être "femme", il faut dire "ça"

unavailable to the expulsive reader who dismisses "absolute" a piece

Tomorrow. Use of this word "wick ears"
ci-haut mentionné. Chaleur de chez nous.
point de repère. The film projected at
elles s'extasent riantes élèvant leurs
verbal pneumae. Inflammatory ruse
illogique, sont des brigandes de la rue
some introductory collusion evident
vagues froides de la mer. Partout
dawn. Pale joints of the body, spiritus
portent les vestons de nylon, c'est à dire
sound "Mont Royal" nocturnal hum of
demeurons ici, facilement, sa dédicace
diminished. Her eyes.
résolue

where so little "actually" fits together, there is no palpable image or whole

La saute de mémoire. Devant l'expiration
nominal. Histrionic, I said, not hyst-

or the "whole" is an elaborate leap of memory, of inner noise &

Civilian decorum she speaks of
courageuse dans le fond la nuit
her arms striking the wall, light
au-delà des collines les nuages
dreamed. Of empirical breath,
lieu de notre rencontre, l'oubli
fixes definitive shapes in spatial
Or nous sommes étonnées, on
insistent, almost physical "dégoût"
ce qui est vertigineusement irréelle
"A. is coming," she called up stairs
le pouvoir des grandes entreprises
must buy or kinesthetic, gaily

she coniferal, abstinent

melody, when what we crave is this: "the woman standing at the lake

Parlant tranquille de. La scène d'épuration
Coral light amplification the basis of oral
de grande souplesse à travers les bras
vibrio lancante tremolo aux aires où
des spectatrices les plus blasées hélent
ailes elles de poussières murmurent la
bondée de tout trou aimable à se livrer
"interregnum." Effronterie ardente

leurre de ses mains, ses épaules ô

silence or sound of hands

the round pebbles underfoot bright grey & eroded play of water"

Anxiety (4 Poems Invented on Trains of the New Jersey Transit Authority Between Princeton Junct. & NY Penn), or Aspen in New York

OHs

When is a word loop not a word loop, when
anxiety fails.
We are at the street corner & the ends of our sleeves
are ohs. Tentatively we put our hands thru them.
A few sentences of ordinary prose make it into the poem,
humming

a few bars. Radio vibrations need a machine with electrodes
or we can't hear, we just run up against these waves
pass thru our chests & arms

which ache, usually, by five p.m.

At a party, we all loop hands & pull the crackers,
unfold the hat of admirals, Queen Obedienca,
Dick Turpin, Ella Fitzgerald's hat too

complete with microphone.

Cricket chirping.

"Fresh* air."

---

*The author is trying hard as usual to be funny. If only she would start with lighter subjects, she wouldn't need to go into such contortions.

SOME STOPS ALONG AN INTERPRETIVE WALK IN NEW JERSEY

People who take trains solely from a desire to register themselves
the desolation of landscape.

Words are permanently in our head but some water is stagnant.

Viewing becomes impossible at a certain range.

Imagine the singing salt being gathered in in nets
& nets.

Later they saw rats running on the cement podiums in the fields.

Sunning themselves or running.

Couriers have driven a long way on the back of cranes.

At certain points, anxiety fails.

From New Jersey, New York appears very small, including the
World Trade Center.

Interminable plus value is not being a felony.

The poisoning of the spirit, or the presence of ambient
noise.

There is a good possibility of giantesses & clowns.

We can stand up & take our cases off the racks now.

Beginning every cicatrice with a "new".

BRINGING AN ASPEN TO NEW JERSEY

for Ken

The brave mountain air.
"Small paper hats have fallen out of the crackers."
There will be leaves in this air.
Blue jays fly up & into the aspens.
It will be amazing just to see it there.
A kind of yellow light would be coming from this aspen.

when we came back to the house
we would see it
glowing

We would make coffee, more coffee
& pull off our anoraks over our heads

People would be standing outside looking at the aspen
citizens of New Jersey & the world
their mouths open, wondering

where did it come from, what is it

We would be inside laughing
& pulling crackers
unfolding the paper lanterns
putting the hats on

The air would be mountain air

NEWHOUSE

Which reminds me of going to school with James Newhouse.
This factor enters into nothing & is meaningless.
I haven't thought of James New hs for years. In fact

there was no Jame Nehs ever, I invented him here
& can make him disappear.

Which rhymes

& I can make that

disappear too*

*We are now completely off the subject of New Jersey. The author has failed
in her task. The electricity bills due to lighting are interminably high & for
what effect; for all her talking, we still have not overcome "the scorched
earth policy." She's fired! There is an opening for a real poet in these pages.

A Grassy Knoll

(GASEOUS CHEMICALS)

To say in America "a grassy knoll"
what is more American than this.

What is more believable than a story of American power.

Not electricity

but power, the power of sadness, the head flung
back & to the left, over & over
"back, & to the left"

& the people running from the corner at the sound of
shooting

american film (shooting)

(NO MONUMENTAL POEMS)

After a while the Americans stopped making monumental poems.

A little of this had to do with positions or territory.
Infraction of the inflated claim to borders.*

A fuel
tank 1/4 empty. Head in the sand "a soldier" his
wire glasses & hair still visible, veteran

Chemist or doctor in civilian life
Having never shovelled snow in Mesopotamia

A service station smells sweet as gaseous chemicals dissipate.
The sign men get down off the ladder, turning off
the apostrophe, &
the music sings *"shimmy shimmy do"*

*Small children were singing on Lenin's hand.

(THE EXISTENCE OF POETRY)

Can poetry alone exist in isolation from*
Can poetry alone exist isolate
Can poetry alone exist in isolation

If ever there is a strengthening daydream
obdurate fences appear above a grassy knoll
a bias slope planted in front of a parking lot

In the apartment
"the pilot light" flickers in the stove, someone
is entering the circle,
we are holding hands around the cards, our dark hair
Bowed

The voice speaks up automatically from the mouth of one of us
(we are not looking who)

*"where the car slowed (~~bitch,~~ he said)"

(MY FELLOW AMERICANS)

,stepping out of the frame

,DTP 065 MTRLTRTO 92/02/11

Television is preempted by announcements of bombs
the president an elderly Causasian (masc.) with a recessive hair gene
"my fellow Americans"
a kind of collegiality
a fraternal organization

In the televised inset the palms
flail their amplitude earthward in the splitting rk rk rk
of machinery, guided by Raytheon, General Electric
whose career ads say "contribute to a dynamic future"

Americans who have never known war on their soil
are numerous, too numerous
& their opinions on war are suspect

their hands are in the armaments industry
their children's mouths

(THE RECOIL)

Later on television the voices are reading the news
"it is the governance of the many by the few" we think
democracy

the recoil of

the green body blown out like a poisoned calf
a pig whose snout is rusting on the hook or ladder
"it is another generation" we think
the head flung back

to the left

back

(under the stress of mortal ammunition stop this, too polemical
"If you don't like this country, go home now"

(PLATES OF RIPE CORN)

How can we get there using closed techniques
Fibre optics light passing

the rail
The passengers just reading their newspapers, sheets folded down
by gravity like dogs' ears
listening
the letters reforming themselves even now
into tomorrow's news
today's with slight variations of syllabic formation
today's with slight vocable familiarity
with anodyne tracers
with lead injected into the blood   *biologically useless*

a new hilarity

the form of this

we are talking of it* over our bhaji lifting
We are talking of it over "plates of ripe corn"

---

*"The part of the state of the union speech that got the most applause is a cut in
the capital gains tax. In the speech, Bush noted that 60% of those who would
benefit earn under $50,000 a year. But the Internal Revenue Service says 72% of
capital gains are reported by people with incomes over $100,000." *(Ken's letter)*

(INSERT PHOTOGRAPH HERE*)

*the saluting boy

(ETERNAL FLAME)

There was a time we looked forth.
Or my uncle the earliest American.

This has no business in the poem, no business.
As if the new continent "America" was a drift or deafening noise.
Later, they returned to Warszawa

A place that encompasses the alphabet
(no form)

The 14-year-old emigrant to Canada, Polish-American.
"Machines, armaments, centurions, machines."
Looking for future

Absolution, not knowing how*&
"winging it"

*Mass at the Assumption of the Blessed Virgin Mary, Tempe AZ

(SOME WISHES)

To insist upon what we are becoming

To become what we insist upon

To wear gilt wings & be known in correspondence as "completely normal"

To smile full-face with bent ears in front of the climbing bars

(blue read yellow blue)

To be part of a huge opulence that has just taken leave

of absence

To wear gilt wings

To be remembered as she who laughed aloud* in "les réunions"

To be recalled as a woman of "warm hands"

To insist upon what we are beholding

To behold what we insist upon:

*Ideas quite naturally here

❖

"The human figure becomes increasingly abstract as it grows older
It is weight not hinge"

— Lyn Hejinian, *Oxota*

Sighs, or The Noise From It

In order to erase from the eons of premeditated distance
the stutter of the arm
The job that is like a blister, put on every day
No one believes it is real
The other half believe it has always existed
A normal part of the body
A sore

In order to palpitate the drum of the chest
like a pediatrician
over the asthmatic girl
her thin chest
the noise from it
A normal part of the body
that has always existed
A crime

In order to operate on the swelling behind the ear
where the brain itself has let go of anguish
into the immune system
Relax
It's not really happening
No one believes in it
Not even the pediatrician
The noise from it

In order to subtract from the annoyances of civilization
a small tablet
an aspirin
This at least, minimally

As we peel off the blister in the darkened room
to lay it down on the dresser beside the bed
& carefully set down the drum of the grown-up chest,
the side of the swollen ear
beside the sleeper who is sleeping,
so as not to disturb her
Tho she occasionally moves her legs as if running sideways
No one believes in it, she's not listening

She's a Palestinian swimming in Lake Ontario
The wave of darkness rising

You can wave back if you like, now

(No one believes it is real)

Devotions

Part of devotion is symmetry, which does not mean what you think, it means hésitation not construct, it means interpellation,* personally, because I said so, I said so.

For "Zorro" the cat

Wherein the thread of a consequence is held up as a mathematical proof.

*"interrupting the order of the day"

Dog Of

Sometimes I think I have a dumb dog of a cat. Pawing old bread
left out as a trap for cats by pigeons, who are smart feathers. All
washed grey & orange. A cat on her knee. Eyes forward, smelling
the old cherry perfecto. Whodunit on the lawn. Squirrel beat.
Frère et soeur.

2

The implication of a red back & orange sides, trimmed up. Ergo sum.

3

Hurling over the far fence, the heavy iron comma.

Fly Out

Where I live an American can fly out a window on a line of poetry, streaming out over the street, then slowing, dropping spent fuel cartridges onto the cars, some ticketed already by the patrols, sailing gently then over the hoods, fence-level, then dissolving, gone. Pigeons that bark like dogs. The absolutely injurious melding of appetites.

2

The cat's flicker beaded up. The nora of it. The red ball.

3

Braquing sudden at the concrete barrier, periods stacked two deep:

Stove On

Sometimes it's her sweater with a kinked-up sleeve, elbow
bent 45 degrees. Reeling back after turning the stove on. An
arm around her "red cat". A tremendous splinter where we
have been born. Grounding the stove. Nose of the cat watching,
flat house we live in.

2

What if I did my dancing standing up, a gaiety in my footstep.

3

Heading at high speed toward the quotation marks.

Space On

There is a lot of space on top of a cat. The pigeons are grey
dogs roughing each other's ears. What is it a bird thinks,
the cat hears. Pacing the window. There is more space over
a cat than under & the birds are hogging it. Holding one leg up
& bowing, bowing. Dog feathers. Pecking at bright glass.

2

A head is a web by which stutters are known. "Bafouille."

3

Bowed in the ICU,* the heart hooked up to the semi-colon.

*I wish she would breathe;

Fear Of

I wake up thinking the word *polio*. People are saying "heart of hearts, heart of hearts." The smallnesses of the understanding are carved into our shoes. Rage of the cat too small to rule a factory, or anyone. Can't say what. *Jest lookit em birds.* Sunning grey top feathers. The last generation to whom the word was fear of bearing, thru a lifetime, the slightly ruined dance.

2

Dirndl. A skirt full of consonants. Epiphenomenon.

3

Why punctuate anything she said makes Art mad the letter Ai

Wire From

Or cat-flounder thru "wet snow", the strings holding any of us
to heaven, a tremendous splinter where we have been born,
crossing the chasm beneath us, a thin wire we could fall from.
Pensive. Cat-jump. A pigeon rotating on its bird spindle.
Freeze-grass in the yard.

2

Walking along its ploughed edge to the small kindnesses.

3

What were they thinking! Pulling the apostrophe thru the head wound?

The Purposes of Skin

"All we want is to explore kindness the enormous
country where everything is silent" J.W.

To raise up the horse, whinnying, dark space of the open
nostril. I am a "person," fearful below hooves.

To play the game where the round bones are shaken in a jar & spilled.
The future depends on this. Children are wailing.

To want to be a deer, to awaken, & want her to touch me.
At the corner, the accordion player in the sun, blind, singing.

Because the eyes miss everything simple, like colour photography they
register *the banal.*

Without touch, I cannot live. Space makes no sense to me,
nor time. The basal ganglia, wanting "love".

To cover the stitched-up holy oak
of the breastbone, where the carvings are, pointing to water.

Trees are a corpus.


```
Trees are a corpus.
Trombones singing the Mass of Ages (shine on me).
A row of grooms up the wedding cake, stopping, thinks
of what Catherine dreams of, these grooms rising up
the trellis, over the fountain of food-dyed water,
falling red like blood.
A leaf shimmers "in paradise".
Her ticket is one minute away.
The noise of the restaurant.
Peoples' bars & stars, they are as usual
getting in & out of U-Hauls. Dragging a cement sofa,
sandbags, literally.
Singing in the trees.
A body finally articulates.
```

Purpose 2

Whose skin smells as if washed with pressed limes.
The deer rears up its head, sharken, eyes

trained on the present pentameter. The movement of her arms.
The sky. It is all one thing to a deer.

The thunder of their sides flashed against the trees. For our eyes
the use of blinders, diminish the visible.

The blind accordion player in front of the bank,
the gizmo chained to him, averting theft of the coin.

The bones are spilled out of the jar, the edge with
2 moons uppermost. The woman touches this.

"An impresario of water," she says.

```
There is a looseness we shall not emulate.
The theatre of the head.
Sheets of loss are knowing too.
Knowing drives the internal mechanism.
Always searching for "solution"
outside the grain of our ordinary
being. Plastic grooms drink the wedding
cake. We walk past the bakery.
The trees of the street are singing.
Pressing one leaf to the top of the head
alleviates the pain.
Where she hit it on the hatchback door.
A body smells of limes & red guava.
Running down her arm.
```

Purpose 3

The paintings of the trees have pointed to water.
The bent night where the deer struck out & tore the sheet

in its shudder. The small screen of TV.
Screen of the head or door she stepped from, energy

screen in the leg or arm, her voice pulled on a thread
thru the sciatic nerve, to the spine

the accordion cycling the air
with its bellows, blindly, I too

am fearful of the hooves, the woman now
lifts her shells, re-reads ocean, a horsehair, a child's palmetto

"Scansion of water, held back by the skin"

Scansion predicates us.
A greed anywhere near us is a stronger surge.
Purpose grinds us over & over.
Individual longing is not ours.
What is & is not taken as serious love,
these atoms are a worry, too.
"Outside" the grain of our ordinary being.
A body smells of smooth lines & trees.
The groceries were in bags a long time in the road.
Even in the snow her insistence was visible.
Urging onward, carrying the letter "a"
which she loves, in the alphabet,
which is "lovable,"
which she also loves.

Purpose 4

A narrow surface delimits the aging hart: the skin
Warm water falls on the back of her head

where beneath the air, the number is, a "courteous life"
she led & regretted deeply later, in the last days

Her voice too a skin, surrounds the inner lake or body

Rubbing up against the deer as she woke,
the grasses flattened beneath her. As if touch makes even

grey light desirable. They wrote together in silence. These too
skins we break through, surface of the hooves

The stove light in the kitchen, her same hands touching
coffee pot, cupboard, stove, bellows

"Endemic," she calls out, "window of
a working prose"


```
Interpreted by glass or windows.
Certain readers elide the "she"s in passages
of love-making, interesting, interesting,
the brain does not recognize what it does not know.
Sheets of touch inside the face are knowing too.
The grooms are rather nice on the wedding cake.
Their plastic bride suits an apparent shunning of
inhibition, or plea to unrealizable safety.
Abstraction feels a little whole.
Interesting details make a story true.
A hand pressed upon the temple.
Still holding her head where she'd hit it "timely"
The guava fell out of the bag when she cried out
Listen, what is it to live in grief or fear
```

Purpose 5

In such a forest (body), the wall or chamber
where the blood is, darkness of the inner spruce

For spruce are dark, pines light & larch are
belief & possibility

& birches are writing, the inventresses of paper
& emotion

which we take into us secretly when we breathe
like a sirop, curing us of our risky aorta

which we never mention, we are so sick of it
(or our skin, which we grew first as a language or paper

our mouths full of amniotic water, resting
oh how I crave that paper

lunge & cry of the deer against the birch or aspen

"forest" of hands

"Noise" of this forest.
Inside our heads, a deterioration or murmur.
We walk past the bakery, in the back there are stored
boxes of sealed plastic archways.
Most emotion is similarly portrayed.
Ease of use is not always desirable, poetry.
Ease of loss is a knowing mechanism too.
An ordinary longing was present in the wedding room,
they stopped shovelling & looked up.
The guava froze on the curb where it fell, she left it.
A corpus of it hinders peripheral seeing.
What drives the head is a tinny mechanism.
She walked past, wearing the red jacket."
Smell of guava inside it, running.
Intractability of inner meaning is a heart song to

Tales of the Sumerians (Auburn, NY)

(eternal darkness)

Sometimes I wake up thinking "rain of blows"
Or are we Sumerian at some point
We remember cuneiform
pressing it (a drug) into damp clay

Words for oil are nothing to us, we know them

Words for trade, for landing on another shore
For wading thru the sands
For clambering upward, the clear blue sky
This is our alphabet
The incubus
Our personhood becomes us the voice of gods in us is still

(the migrations)

But an ache in it, the cortex aching
Is it the beginning or the end of heaven
I have come in on something started long before me
have entered the long hall of cerebral pathways
exalted
maybe
I have taken a step & bear with me the tools of work, of kitchens
bear with me my youth tho it is phantom-slim
The hall is great its mortar groans between the stones
I have only a small ancestral waking
only the triangular words
My ancestor an emigrant, mute at first
The key to all the stories
stony silent
standing in the photo behind the husband, behind the sons
her dress is satin, shimmers
Two jars of oil, a sheaf of barley
A great extravagance, no one remembers
A stony silence
The seventh dynasty she has lived thru to get here, this far, a page
The syncope of narration

Held back, a kind of weather
The hail beating down upon the crops & men forever
My grandfather standing with the fawn & bottle
"We bore her off in the great wood coffin"
"rain of blows"

Halls

There are motions of the earth in which everything
is forgiven

No one of us is built to earthquake standards

The way they later shored up train stations with their huge halls
of air

that had to be kept perfectly still
while the story was being told

New steel beams cut into the walls & bolted

Snap shirts with a gold filament running down the sleeve
as if the arm had been addressed by a tongue

writing from the shoulder to the wrist

Fault-line by which others can enter the body
by accident

You turning toward me, for instance

one of those motions

a forest tipped

was singed

you turning this way

the Okanagan valley

Oregon

Highway 9

the tributaries of the Amazon

STARS

Waiting out the *grand hall de la gare* with a ticket
to a tributary
A few packages, a lung with writing, a sling of fruit or shoes

My ticket bearing the name of your arm
the one that I invented
to touch you

your eye on me as I move inland, my head bowed
forgiven everything

later holding my mouth close to the stars, waiting for the voice to echo out
"Matapédia"

salmon rising in the blue dawn
visible

the Amazon, lights of the city earthbound on another shore

Your return

to the Belmont exit

an "injury to the canoe"

red dawn

Albuquerque

One of those motions

the coast of Oregon

a forest wailing

culled steel in the outer wall

ARROYO

But the gold thread of the shirt I have been wearing
along my arm
that line where I can be opened up like a canyon or arroyo

where wild & harrowed dogs live
plants fires   stones "symmetrical over time"

planets with radiant spokes or bulged equators

you can descend this canyon, unto the waters
drink of its earthly darkness

magnetic pattern of the earth echoed in the poles of the body

& climb back safe
to the hall of the train station

where breath is

(the reed wet)

my arm held up

A lake & tower

a river of fresh snow

Highway 9

vehicle of ponderance

light jacket

us inside it

Oregon

Your turn to me

SPILL

Turns of the planets which spill outward into space
asymmetrical

For instance:
the flutter of the heart on the left side of the body

Carried everywhere into the air of train stations
That must be held so still

because all of us are moving
& may detonate the earth at any moment

approaching (too close) a fault-line
concatenated pressure in the floor of the planet

the thread of gold on a shirt I have been wearing
Filament from the heart to the wrist-bone's portal

shirt-snaps touching the tunnel into the hand

(σομε υνυσεδ ωορδσ, φορ Γαιλ)

pertinent

trésorier

pineal

range road

fescue

watercourse

signal-fire

dome

Halls

We who have lived between air & the air
stationary

Who have divided the air with our bodies
a mathematics, an axiom

a canyon   a dome

So that we too may receive the calibration of air
in the immense hall of the train station

As we bow down readying the wrist & shoulder
Admitting in ourselves the fault-line of the planet

the hand raised to us in anticipation or forgiveness

Oh the hand, "by this hand I name you"
in which, the rivers . . .*

*she is last seen in white water, raising her paddle, preparing to lunge it
downward into the current, with all the force of the latissimus dorsi, sprung
outward, tensile, the earthquake . . .

❖

"And then there's explaining. What does explaining do?
Explaining takes up space. It convinces even one way or the
other. Explaining begs trust. It makes up for actions we would
have intended if we had known better how. Explaining is an aside.
Or what about avoiding explaining? Like in poetry."

— Alan Davies, *Carla*

Reasons of State

They voted for an increase in social order
they voted for an increase in social order
they voted for an increase in social order

The fabric of it rent
in two
Now you have damaged the cloak, said the accuser

A bird we raise An internal action

Uncoupled now in the head
& abolished
I can't think so
I can't think otherwise

A version of the polemic
resists speaking

Impertinence denies fuel for mental being
The fuel tanks are heating

A version of the polemic
calls out

A version of the polemic

Stop this poison
Stop this poison
  "   "   "

Or Exemplary

"Il faudrait changer ce mot ridicule; cependant la chose existe."
— *Stendhal*

What is an anger but a very verse. A bridge with its two towers falling inward.
The five defenders who died on this bridge. I am not, then, "ethnically
clean". It is human frailty tape-looped on the
screen, the medieval bridge falling inward

We can play it backward the bridge at Mostar can rise again.
We can play it backward.
In our head the tape moves back, it is "scene on scene"
The still river erupting upward into smoke & sticks
The stones rising into towers
The reddened syrup coiling fast into the woman's neck
which inflates a head & lifts up, mouths *liebling*

Le coup.
Le souffle coupé.
Le coup de souffle.
De foudre.

You saying "a reall pain in the ass"

The bridge crumbling downward again under the mortar blast.
In the head one bears the name "denouement" into the concrete road
A look, mine or yours
It is cinema too, play this look backward

But are we human
But are we human
But "   "   "
  "   "   "   "
  "   "   "   "

Or exemplary
Or shining knights
Or "prevail"
Or "Greater (insert name of country here)"

Torrid

A douleur is exciting but what is it near
The ecology of a text is such that

The blades or platters of the leaves
A serious start at life's tomorrow
An arpeggio, drastic as it may seem
I slept, dreaming of the Japanese mother & crossing borders
Physically it was hotter, torrid
Perception is acute on first awakening
Sympathetic response is a nervous behaviour
Clocking the coffee
A hotter
Waking
If it wasn't a wound it would be funny
Flying
Said was

The sign an arbitrary wave, as is the cigarette
held in the mouth by a boy
Interesting is a caveat here
Punctilious a word that applies to you, your honour
Or noded in gold leaf paint beneath the arches
Why not swims a better day
Realizable

Every thing has its habit or
douleur

It is ever a usual way to live
We are waiting it
Heat or *canicule*
Obus

Awaiting the onset of summer heat 7a.m.
A heady feeling
Thinking of cunnilingus performed by a girl
Shiver

The mortar shells elsewhere landing on the bisected ville
Interpretation, as if the cigarette
A small car landing is not a belief
Drudgery, she said, describing housework

The wind comes in through the holes of trees
Into the house, I mean
What she said is incomprehensible
Outside

An ever is usually what we do seek
Our every move wanders it
Few achieve or culminate

Accomplishment is a fake disorder

Appreciative
Preying or harps

A government saying it makes it usual
At the same time not acceptable

A sight of the tidal bore in memory

At the same time not acceptable

At the same time not acceptable

At the same time not acceptable

At the   "   "   "   "

   " "   "   "   "   "

   " "   "   "   "   "

Parts of a Clock, or Asthma

> *Two years into the Bosnian civil war, on February 5, 1994,*
> *a mortar shell fired into Sarajevo market killed 68 Saturday*
> *shoppers.*

The poem is not a
cute thing. Thousands of us have vanished into there.
Perished. Or.

A woman has come to sell parts of a clock. A small
ramshackle table is set up where she waits with the clock piece.

A description of attire. Who is wearing what
in this picture. Where the black leather coat is. The
dream of - - - - - - - - this Saturday before the shell hit.

Killing 68.* The poem is not a cute
thing. Wearing the "manteau de voyage".

The available supply of goods diminished

---

*A war cannot be put into a poem.

2) Fatty-acid

A defect in fatty-acid metabolism
leaves us fearful. The woman is not in the market

a hole in the buildings opposite. Trailers of goods exist in the
head where they rumble at the border check-points

priests counting the alcohol. "Their yellow beards
are long & the drivers are cold, waiting."
This is what the woman's head is saying in the market,
so alive, a conscious spark or glow in the universe
this living

Or a hot firefly over the hay fields of Garthby Québec could be
as nuanced, as fine

An investment in emerging Latin markets over the next 2-3

3) Chest-level

An examination of the shell crater leaves us wondering.
The northeast hills it came from, killing 68.*
Its gentle nose, they said, struck

the market table, exploding in mid-air at chest-level, the iron
sleeve shattering with the charge & propelling shards
at rocket-speed, still audible,

shearing the bodies. A clock broken is these pieces. Some clocks still
for sale here. The never-ending repetition of markets.
Someone needs what someone else might have,
or we exchange nothings. Circulation in the broken stands.

The crucible. We meant to

Increased consumption is possible in a zero-based

---

*in Sarajevo, not the poem.

4) Description of asthma

A metabolic cue or error. Her endometrium
concentrates arachidonic acid. The woman dreams of

bread & laughs, secretly. Who are we apart from this inner spark
whose neural screen or glow makes "bread"? The wounds
in the buildings & towers she walks thru.
Opens the blood supply of the organism,
irrevocably.

Others bring the found jacket to the market,
the old piece of iron, someone can boil it, or shoes.
A woman wants to bargain these old clock parts of time for

shorn at chest-level. 68 minus 1. An end to it here*

~~Recurrent attacks of shortness of breath, cough & expectoration of~~
~~tenacious mucoid sputum~~

In the long-term, market corrections are largely irrelevant to

---

*there is no more "endometrium". The poet has no right to use it. She has split a
gut laughing. Out of the slice, they took the fibrous organ. She said yes yes yes to
the pain meds.

Brief & Fragile (A History of Reading)

Tic, a door.

Amazement in the first book of the alphabet.

Orange.

A soaring life.

A physical relation to the text, to text; to Texual gates[1]

"Rebattable", liking the quickening in the head, a purr.

False gesture leads to the false self.

~~Emperial Isosceles evident.~~

Certain non-negotiable positions, carefully blurred.

The pictured uses of Scotch™ tape, to whom does this refer?

What a good book needs is more good books, is good shelving.

It is an absolute posture, the belief in the author's voice.

A glance of a mad cat. A mad glance.

Some trust has just been invented here.

Impasse due to cars from the previous light still in the intersection.

A river, cold water over cold stones.

Inroads were made in the discussion.

The pictured uses of scotch tape on the dispenser, to whom does this culturally refer?

A craniate being at moins trente centigrade, wearing two overcoats.

The creation of experience is what the brain *does*.

---

[1] The cattle can't cross, & watch us, their sides steaming

The word "cold". Or any other.

The act of reading is a bead on the perceptual circuit, triggers the bead of abstract thought.

Certain signals must cross here.[2]

The sender-receiver-feedback model is obsolete, a pattern of paternal obstinence, it forgets "culture", forgets *white noise.*

Sniggering under the cuff of.

Critical endeavour fails to catch up.

There was a palpable groan in the room when the subtitles came on.

Pine sap rubbed on her ear as a palliative measure.

Cortical splendour.

Reading is a cortical splendour

How do you love me is a rose.

Delirium of (we say) *the white-tailed deer.*

2 Estuary

A permutable life. In 1971 or any other, the sun warming the rough wall wherein the sea. O riven malice. That one word follows another, significance. A history of cultivation followed the great western migrations. A concept of "person", without which "time" is not possible. They had crossed the Atlantic in boats to escape the armies. The light of the American motel as we walked back down the road. She laughs.[3] The towel falls. (We had been swimming.) It's a big joke. Today there are immigration laws.[4] Sky struck, open

---

[2] Textual gates

[3] An in-joke about cattle, or "my horse, King"

[4] But this is a history of reading. Even the horse King only exists in memory; for the rest of us, he is "my horse, King".

For Mitterand's Life, For My Life, For Yours

I am drinking history into my mouth. Going down
it makes a sound like "beauty, beauty".

The convergences of what we have not seen of what *is*.

A massive tree growing in the spirit, not catalpa, oak, fir, eucalyptus

scission, inner scission.

2

The president seen in the photograph of the far-right demonstrators
in 1935. Another there who heard their cries said the words were:
"down with the filth of foreigners (Jews)". But he, he
does not remember.

Is it so hard to remember?
Is it so hard to be the person one once was, de l'assumer sur
les épaules de "maintenant"?
Is there still a thing: the purity of Frenchness?

3

A massive tree growing in the heart, in the darkness or street
under the curved lamp, in sleep, in the limbs
Where my name is, a tree is growing

Silence is the name of such a tree, its weight chokes, oh oaken beauty, oh elm,
history is such "beauty"

we dream of:
Bulldozers ripping the grey stones of the dead.
Making a parking lot. The building behind is a video store.
All the brothers are in the hotel at the road, behind immense vehicles,
seeking the white bird
seeking the white animal that vanished into the wheel

4

While I am inside wanting "sexual love", if that is love
but there are no women in this dream
They are somewhere else sewing tricolor flags
They are waiting to shout their own slogans
I don't want to hear, unless it is "vulva, vulva"
I don't want to hear it, unless

The roots of the tree pass down into the arms I feel these roots
The roots of the tree shimmer in the hands I feel these hands
The leaves are the surface of an ocean

5

I am drinking this ocean like history into my mouth. Going into the stream
my mouth makes a noise. This is beauty. I want you.
The jets have left us & I have landed near you. *This is beauty.*
This is age. This is presence. This is the book of first laws.
To know this. This is beauty.*

---

*If she thinks she can fucking get away with this, she is crazy. Sex is not an escape
hatch from poetic difficulty. There is still a thing, damn it: the purity of Frenchness.
Is it so hard to remember? That we struggled so hard against this scourge to save
you? *It is we, the dead, who were the first readers.*

❖

"Terrain trains the mind's recognition of its own
surroundings.
She found
                    herself again.
Stained glass rosettes roll in howling
with faith."

— Lise Downe, *A Velvet Increase of Curiosity*

Screaming

in memorium S.D.

When I think "damp footprints" the girl runs toward me in the snowy yard

a fur collar risen upward

sunbeam against her face & hair on 36th Avenue

the day my father took the pictures

a knitted hat was tied at my smallest brother's chin

smothered in small stitches

stepping up on the same cracked stairs now

no event whatsoever provides me memory

trigger absolute

the mind "forgets"

in the photo we are stood by the car like happy siblings

an insistence invented by light that very moment

no one shouts at anyone now or in the future

no one rants at us

my smallest brother laughing, laughing

his expression of satisfaction at such a laughter

us looking sideways at his face & tied hat

his round head under that & small devoted ear

the scar on his chin from falling downstairs

for a few minutes he lay so still forever

then got up, screaming

Paris *n*Sleep

The year I moved from the blue coast to rue Jeanne-Mance
"François Truffaut" died.
We are all full of our hostage selves.
In the U.S. of America he would have been

Frank Tranfield. The polished surface of
the piano, as usual. "The man gets up."*
His small name is Frank Trout, short for Francisco Tiriani.

He is fifty-two years old & there is a bridge of thin blue metal
over his black granitic tablet,* the shine of it

"Tripoli agonistes persepolis free."

* *

*People are always getting up in these poems.
*Frankly, the reference is obscure. Say "grave in Montmartre."

The year I moved to Paris, the parade of the
Trocadéro. School children got up, dressed
like clowns. "Children"

because they remember so many prior centuries.
One has coal sideburns & a moustache,
climbs the Butte under full adult escort.

Is this how we are teaching children?
Already they are dressed up as someone
other than themselves.
Brighter.
More like the moon.

More like us, who have no childhood.

========================

*where the sewing machine was thrown

"The saints" she thinks, & gets up. Lace tablecloths.
Every place, plaza, praça, piazza, square, carré

is trying to grow four (4) trees.
These trees can be multiplied later by
other trees (x) in order to arrive at

the total number of trees (n).
The world (while we are sleeping)
is held together by this

simple, positive (*)

arithmetic.

)))

*our hostage faces

La femme qui traverse la rue cet après-midi de novembre
looks like Hélène Gauthier ten years ago in Vancouver

but ain't

due to a neat trick: linear
time.
The grilles of the windows & high potted chimneys, burnt red
dans le quartier Médard ou n'importe quel
quartier

This fall, the last eyeful of Paris those
square stone towers over the sleeping Mont Ste. Geneviève.
5 a.m., she gets up alone, turns her back &

walks toward the trees of the Luxembourg, no, the
Luxembourg "RER"

* *

*Comparing colours (the flowers, say) to noise.

Sleep to the (n)th power: the two trees
of the Place de la Contrascarpe
Verlaine with one ear on his pillow
sleeps just like the rest of us
in a room over the rue Descartes

he hears the ocean rising up to clean
the Paris gutters.*

Later he gets up & goes outside, his collar up (it's November 7)
& has coffee in a white cup.
Reading in the old book: "foot-scape," "eider,"
"sylvan," "toreador."

The restaurants just now across the street*

opening

+++++++++++++++++++++++++++

*mélée of the road below the hotel, an accidental
*the waiters outside in new aprons, lifting the long shutters

Absolutely a ground zero.
Infamy. Laughter from the white door 31.

The old tap of wine, behind the zinc.
"still screen"

Screen cortical, this. The conscious
examination of "this cortical screen."

Ten years of sleep "out of sync" with
the time zone. Blip abscess,* worn out.

No visual image remembered, just the skin on
the inside of the arms.

She gets up, sleep on her skin, tearing
the hôtel winding-sheet*

∧ ∧ ∧ ∧ ∧ ∧ ∧ ∧ ∧ ∧ ∧ ∧ ∧ ∧ ∧ ∧ ∧ ∧ ∧ ∧

*Infamy in Paris, or *Ricard* before dinner, the lights coming on. People
are always getting up in these poems, it's an irritant to the lyric whole.
*Maybe in another lifetime Mouré will smarten up. A good title
might be "Polishing Up the Abrasions".

4 Translations from Rilke

For my friends

1) TRANSMONTANO[1]

A note is in the soup
Cows are too

We don't know how to liquor it now
Friendly or "Beast!"

Is a word translated still a word?
Un mot traduit est-il encore un mot?

The soup is bottomless anyhow, a real pot
So button your collar up before going under

Why aren't you blowing your shoulder out
like the lamp beside you

letting it get cold

2) TRIESTE[2]

In the dream, in particular
I was in charge (it seemed) of "italics"

Syllables in Rome
or, their theory

"Dessinance", which meant
I had to draw painstakingly each syllable by hand

It was only the declension
of the verb "employment"

& could endure

We were both standing out in your yard at night
under the huge pines

I was so surprised at "perspective"

The umbrella was shorter than the stars

3) BAR S[t.] LAURENT[3]

We were speaking that night on a sort of altar
cut into the lip of the Mountain

A bazaar table covered with a white cloth & clips
Me, then you
Your topic was "narrational presence"

You were serving cups of something, little paper ones,
Salsa, I think
Lined up as offerings

A kind of green one you'd chopped up with jalapeños
onion & coriander
(I was nervous)

People were holding these cups in their fingers
& sipping gently

I was going to speak on the "Czech" or "check" shirt
After these refreshments

4) AUX DEUX MAGOTS[4]

When you rang, I was thinking of
places I could kiss you
in Paris

Your neck, at the point above the top of your shoulder
where the sweater pulls sideways
with the strap of your small packsack

as you turn your head on the way out of 19, rue des Imaginés

nodding to the concièrge in the unlit hallway
A Pole who had married a German once & now lives in darkness
(une femme à ne pas provoquer)

The door blazing with ordinary grey sunlight
a few feet away

Bonjour

Key to restaurants:

[1]The Transmontano was a Portuguese corner restaurant on Roy 3 blocks
east of the Main, now made over as Else's. In my job, we once got a letter
from a customer (whose only custom was writing letters) that began
"Beast! Beast! Beast!"

[2]The Trieste is in Disraeli, Québec, on the shore of Lac Aylmer. It has
awful paintings of Roman ruins, but when you step out of it at night, you
can see the stars. This section is for Mary di Michele, whose backyard
and patio umbrella are in the poem. "Dessinance" is clearly "dissonance"
heard wrong, however, in the dream, "employment" really was a verb.

[3]The Bar. St. Laurent is above La Cabane on the Main and is here
because some sectors would have me stop writing so badly about the
Main. In deference to them, this poem is not about the Main. I only
threw the name in to get their backs up.

[4]Aux Deux Magots is in Paris on the boul. St. Germain. It is full of
people who have been drinking coffee or seltzer since WW2.

❖

"And when her hands were put back on they were backwards, in argument with the institutions, in evidence of life, evacuation, the product perceived as work, designated to the other. Incidents are objects."

— Norma Cole, *My Bird Book*

Tonic

"Description bounds a person's life."
Lyn Hejinian

She looks at me thru her cataracts
A disease develops slowly

There are clouds in the sea over Amsterdam

A trace of blood is in the bitter soil
Its remembered taste accompanies everywhere

All my life I am beginning to account for
the fact of immigration

Not belonging here on the surface but at the end
of the wire

Treasure hopeful

Abstinence

2

What is not & is a factor
This is "disequilibrium"

this or "tonic"

A modality we cannot express except thru
daily labour
Pansies when we get home looking up at us

Okay
I'll go back then tomorrow

3

So we work at it slavishly & come back
I will do or I will do so

Noise like this is human consciousness

The difference is always an intricate sense of measure
We are working beings
propelled by natural wonder

Where we do not have a vicious insight into balance
Public "strikes" are civic savings

It is fiscal effacement
(we are our own impediment walking the soil of)

4

In the shirt or eye, bearing
Already we have come thru an exhausted waking

Her eyes are blurred, the lens is cloudy
Immediate assertion brings relief

Dialogue begins a way of saying
We talk & talk is "tonic"

They sew it inward in the operation

5

As long as the fact exists, what must account for it
A purpose is gleaned from the centre of endeavour

A fetishization of visual areas
Or anticipation

If ever a roof was making us anonymous
a woman's name is Anastasja

The purple & yellow heads are blurred among the leaf stems
We are obedient to small plants therefore

Relief is possible

6

Thru the cloud the kitchen sink shimmers
One slip of foot & stone abrades the skin

O daughter

Interpretive choosing is not a way of glamour
but anticipation

the papers, oranges, shoe
A view of rocky mountains tipping downward
from the kitchen window

The sad lawn of parks develops memory
People below us like small bellows

inebriate

(it is factual)

7

Because of cloud, our descent is ever slower
"the east slope was rough with intrusive shale"

If the clouds are over Amsterdam
we wait in the room to see its rising

Since we have come to sit, the fact is older
Fewer assertions conduct us to relief

When she walks I know
I am the answer to an immigration

The others below us wave her downward
The doctor there already dressing for the operation

O patient women

Our promise silent
"not yet"
Ever we have done so

When the poem ends, if you remember, is Nelson Eddy singing "without a song"

Nureyev's Intercostals

We all have our altars & icons.
"Nureyev's intercostals." Their instrument
we carry in our head

she said. Obedient to the last "ladder."

Cold chest derivative of air. Or:
cold chest, derivative of air.

Thusly, thusly, days, months, *atonement.*

Chest freezers. Mastic. Stick-on breast stickers.
Chest of drawers.*

@

Oh, be sure to make sense in
another lifetime. Tip coffee from the hot stove,
to be lucky we have a "hot stove"

"seems obvious." The verb precedes its object,
its correlative, its relation
by intention or knowledge of the body,
the epistemological

sense of it. Like this poem

---

*Her chest faced east.
"Up several times in the night with asthma."

%

or don't, who cares. "Writerly majesty goes
nowhere." A fleet air enters
the scroll of the lungs, the bag of the lungs, the
wet albumin (trumpet) of the lungs.

Wind carved into a hill's brow.

There is, she said, *your heart wherein*
fiction lives, fed by the lungs.
Oh, stop
talking about the lungs!

@

What I have learned & not learned from
"Phyllis Webb."

Obedient hours spent in front of the words, finding
my mouth has a hole in it, neatly
mended, leading
out of the face, where else, idiot.**

I get up, shouting, no one is here!
Mouthpiece. Slattern. Obvious

**". . . among birds the (excision) of one member of the pair leads to a search
with abnormal manifestations that can last for days. Some of the symptoms of
depression may derive from search procedures — attempts to establish new
connections between brain activity and a changed environment." Rosenfeld, *The
Invention of Memory*, p. 65.

\#

Am I a monster, or is this what it means
to be a person? Reading this is, reading
"Clarice Lispector." Quotes around a name.

But Nureyev? Those amazing intercostals!
Beads of bodily light!
Side lunges, sit-ups, leg raises can't imitate them!
To make a script out of the body.
Read my torso's frontal fiction

"Clarice" "Phyllis"

@

Or: a day in Lisbon. Walking in the green
jacket, "jauntily" shall we say, she is
that flicker.

Thru the Almada quarter, old roofs
& shutters, shut. Loose laundry.

History of fish, pulled up out of
the water.

"Gail."

%

What can make us believe? The space
where belief is?

Where we invented it, calling up
the future tense, the verbs "getting old with,"
their cerebral tracing

Light on the face of, her face.
Typanum & violin.

Without her, the imagination is
torn from its future formulations. Leaving
silent music.

"Typanum & violin."

@

for Jon Whyte

"In some cases a lethal dosage
is necessary to remove pain."
The wall of the barn cracking so loud
they woke up & ran into the dirt driveway.

The back half of it fell.
When they saw*** it, they stood up, she stood up

& held our ribs in.****

***"Said."
****This is an impossible sequence of pronouns. Try again "her chest hurt."

%

Bearing the internal catastrophe, irremediable.
"3 nuns stepping out of a Toyota."

Just yesterday, on the road in the université McGill,
their black coats & skirts & wings. A wine smear.
In the side of the head, un couteau.

Ça couteau trop cher, imaginez ça, donc, chérie
these uncontrollable colours I have spoken of,
trop dispendieuses,
trop crasseuses,
I who have painted colours, these

(these signs)

for which there are
"no other uses"*****

—————————————————

*****Her hands, holding her ribs in. Later, the mask of breath,
her chest faced east. Several. O Gail. "Writerly majesty goes nowhere."

Dream of the Towns

I've been getting over a shaved pudenda
I've been playing the bagpipe of the intestines
& what have I learned
apocrypha

Then, I was in a hospital window high over Montréal
I called it my penthouse & lay in the horizon six days, for six days
they helped me rise up
& commit to memory my vital signs

Now I am just left of the alley where the weedy tree blooms its blossomy
leaves, sleeping face-down in shadowy afternoons
I thank you everyone for your dream of the towns
where you saw me, running wildly

Valença do Minho, Chlebowicz, Duga Res

As for me I am abstinent awhile yet

The tremour still here

      (the slice in me

Notes:

1) Valença do Minho is a northern Portuguese border town, directly across the Minho (Miño) from Tuy, in Pontevedra province, Galicia, España.

2) Chlebowicz is the birthplace in Poland, now in the Ukraine, of the author's mother. It may have a different name now.

3) The residents of the town of Duga Res in Croatia in 1992 or 1993 cut down a wood of 88 trees they themselves had planted to honour Marshall Tito's 88th birthday, saying they were removing "the last remnants of the communist regime."

May 17, 1994

The Notification of Birches

CUSTOMS   *for Gail*

I am thinking about *the fact of essences*
played out in the theatre of disbelief

There is a sense in which poetry cannot tell
the truth about anything

Except to say
"before us there is a birch forest"

As opposed to prose
where there are truly essences

Persons, respositories of belief
without whom the rest of us are nothing

we stand absolved

the birch forest astounds us who are accustomed
to "aspens"

the white trunks of the "bouleau" in autumn
out there

or deer

SENSE

There is a sense in which
poetry is not the notification of anything

abrupt

the acknowledgement of peaceable discontinuity
in our lives

a storm of which is remaindered
grass sticking out of it
the beach houses held shut with plywood

over which, the layers of the wind
painted with a thick brush-stroke

(how can we exceed this with werdtsz)

COATS

In particular, the coats we drape to make the cold turn back
wordless

out there with the constellation Orion
who is falling slowly, shield downward

where does the cold go when we do not let it into our bodies
our small wings we could have grown & failed

There is a sense in which it is no good to
talk so clearly about a "life" in poetry

or the way it feels writing this
(should I say so?)

Those wings withered & small in the space under the arm
Between this arm & the central body

The furnace
or pen

Talk instead about the constellation tipping slightly
Talk instead about the line of expressiveness

ECONOMY

If you held a pen under the arm to read the temperature
of the next strophe

A periodical leafed through & abandoned against a tree
is "garbage" but becomes us

Women in the workforce are forces of immediate expression
of the economic foundation of existence

of self
the economy of being

there is a sense in which poetry fails to exercise
the faculties fully

due to the lull in the head brought on by tiredness
(birches represent "amazement" here)

LANGUAGE

Or the birches represent amazement
having been swept forward

& up
Out of the imagined river

legally blind or incapacitated & waiting for a chair
the essence of "being"

Use-value, usefulness are in the saying
we do not know this or anything otherwise

or still

They turned us upside down & shook us
held us up like fish

we knew then there is a "world of spaces"
moral value

we came from the culture of fishes beforehand
the teeming at certain rocks excites us truly

thought is sediment, laid down, beautiful

a r yp al oï

Acknowledgements (found, surely)

Thanks to Lou Nelson for *son soutien constant*, to Anna Isacsson for good humour and clear intelligence, to Robert Majzels for reading the first draft of this work and offering incisive comments (lighting inner arguments), to Phil Hall, to my staff at VIA for their unwavering belief, I like that, to my brother Ken for what he stands for, to the word "désir" winking in the form of stars (*cure our sentences*), and to Maryse Pellerin for quoting me the phrase: "La question possède une force que la réponse ne contient plus."

Thank you to the editors of the magazines in which these poems have appeared: *Arc, Border Crossings, Canadian Forum, Colorado Review, Crash*, CV2, *Paper Guitar (A Descant Reader), filling Station, Prairie Fire, Quarry, Tessera, The Malahat Review, This Magazine*, and *West Coast Line*.

Search Procedures, or Lake This was first published as a chapbook by DisOrientation Books, Calgary, for which I thank Nicole Markotic and Ashok Mathur.

Je veux parler tout simplement de l'amour inconditionnel. Aimer quelqu'un inconditionnellement, c'est ça pour moi la liberté. La liberté personnelle, la liberté absolue. D'avoir la capacité d'aimer quelqu'un inconditionnellement est la racine même de la liberté. Et c'est ça que je vous souhaite, chère lectrice, cher lecteur.